WOULD YOU RATHER

HALLOWEEN EDITION

300+ CREEPY CRAWLY QUESTIONS & ACTIVITIES FOR A GHOSTLY GOOD TIME

EMERALD MAROON

Special Art

Would You Rather – Halloween Edition
300+ Creepy Crawly Questions and Activities for a Ghostly Good Time

Cover Illustration by Renata Souza

This book is intended for entertainment purposes only. Some questions describe exaggerated or fictional scenarios and should not be attempted in real life.

Published by Special Art Books
www.specialartbooks.com

Paperback ISBN: 9791255534013

Name:

____

Date Started:

____

Are you ready to face some scary, silly, and haunting Halloween questions?

CONTENTS

INTRODUCTION

Hi, I'm Goolia the Ghost . . . about to take you through a spooky collection of questions to get you ready for Halloween! One of my favorite things about this day is that you can be anyone, and there is no limit on how funky your ideas can be.

This book is full of questions that will ask you to think outside the box and get creative! What are your favorite things? What scares you? What makes you laugh? What do you love? What annoys you?

Along the way, you'll also develop your opinions, ideas, perspective, and get to know yourself and others on a deeper level through your silly answers. Let these questions inspire you to use your imagination and explore the world around you with curiosity and wonder.

This book is often most fun with a friend or family member, when you can see how different your choices are! So invite your favorite people to dive in with you.

In the following pages, you'll explore the candy dilemmas, costume chaos, haunted houses, ghostly surprises, monster mayhem, and more!

Get ready to get creepy and cool as you decide:

What would you rather?!

TIPS FOR GROUP PLAY

Using this book for group play is all about understanding each other in new ways. Every answer is an insight into the person you play with . . .

- What do they love?
- What scares them?
- What makes them laugh?
- What do they dream about?
- Did anyone's answers surprise you? If so, how?

Let the questions and your answers ignite a new level of friendship and connection with those you play with.

It's not a competition; instead, it's a time to learn more about those around you and what makes them unique.

1.

CREATURE TRANSFORMATIONS

It's time to transform into
a creepy creature yourself!
The only question is,
what would you rather?

WOULD YOU RATHER...

have spider legs

OR

ogre hands?

grow a third eye like a Cyclops

OR

vampire fangs?

transform your ears into furry ones like a werewolf

OR

have a split tongue like a lizard?

WOULD YOU RATHER...

grow a pointed tail like a devil

OR

whiskers like a kitten?

have chicken feet

OR

only be able to bark when you speak?

grow wings out of your back

OR

be able to melt into a puddle
like a jelly monster?

WOULD YOU RATHER...

be able to turn invisible

OR

become a magic wand when casting spells?

have your head shapeshift into a pumpkin

OR

your skin into a mummy's cloth rolls?

learn to shapeshift by the light of a full moon

OR

with a magical puff of smoke?

WOULD YOU RATHER...

be a creature that has tiny bugs crawling out of your eyes

OR

your mouth?

cackle and turn invisible

OR

scream boo and levitate?

grow glowing eyes out of the tops of your feet

OR

have your voice transform into high-pitched screams?

WOULD YOU RATHER...

be the only spooky creature friend in a group

OR

have a spooky creature friend but you're human?

sneeze and bring a zombie creature up from their grave

OR

burp and turn yourself into a fire-breathing dragon?

giggle and shapeshift into a fairy with wings

OR

grow a mermaid tail whenever you get wet?

WOULD YOU RATHER...

haunt your best friend as a spirit

OR

haunt your parents?

build your own creatures in
a transformation cave

OR

wake up as a creature experiment
yourself like Frankenstein?

become a devilish doll with
stitches across your face

OR

a real-life walking scarecrow?

WOULD YOU RATHER...

shapeshift into a raven when you jump from a ledge

OR

become a slime creature when you smell candy?

turn into a bat and ride around on your best friend's shoulder

OR

a rat and cling to their hair?

MIDNIGHT MAGIC STORY CHAIN

1. Grab a pen and paper (or use a notebook) so you can keep track of your spooky tale.
2. One player starts by writing (or saying) the opening line: "At midnight, I transformed into . . ."
3. Going around in a circle, everyone adds one new sentence to the story.
    - Be as silly or spooky as you like!
    - Examples:
        - "Then I grew bat wings!"
        - "My pumpkin head started glowing!"
        - "The black cat whispered a secret to me!"
4. No idea is too wild. The stranger the twist, the better!
5. Keep going until everyone has had at least two turns, or until the group agrees the story feels finished.
6. At the end, read the whole story out loud from start to finish for lots of laughs (and maybe a few shivers!).

EXTRA OPTION

Illustrate the story with a quick drawing of the funniest or spookiest moment.

GROUP PLAY

CREATURE MIX-UP DRAWING

1. Get a piece of paper and some pens or pencils. Fold the paper into three sections (top, middle, bottom).
2. The first player draws the head of a creature in the top section. When finished, fold the paper so no one else can see the head.
3. The second player draws the body in the middle section. Fold it again to hide the drawing.
4. The third player draws the legs, feet, or tail in the bottom section.
5. When everyone's done, unfold the paper to reveal your brand-new, silly, never-before-seen creature!

EXTRA CHALLENGE

Give your creature a funny name, write a short description of its magical powers, and a creepy fact about them or their favorite snack.

2. COSTUME CREATIONS

Halloween is a time when you can become anyone or anything you want! It is the perfect celebration to let your imagination run wild with ideas. The only question is, ***what would you rather?***

WOULD YOU RATHER...

dress up like a fairy princess
with wings and a tutu

OR

a robot that can electrocute people?

invent a glow-in-the-dark skeleton suit

OR

a candy dispensing machine that leaves
a trail of sweets wherever you walk?

wear a pirate eye patch

OR

stormtrooper helmet?

WOULD YOU RATHER...

accessorize your costume
with a wizard's wand

OR

a gladiator's shield?

dress up as a pony with a long mane

OR

a piglet with a curly tail?

be a gargoyle with stone wings and
be pulled around on a trolley

OR

an evil clown with a crazy laugh?

WOULD YOU RATHER...

create long, dangly spider legs that hang off a skirt and swing around you

OR

slime that you cover your whole body with and is gooey to the touch?

use your make-up skills to draw fake scars like a zombie

OR

scales like a lizard creature?

dress up as a character from your favorite movie

OR

favorite music band?

WOULD YOU RATHER...

be something creepy

OR

cute for Halloween?

dress up as a scorpion with a tail that stings

OR

a furry yeti from the mountains?

build wings to be a phoenix
bird rising from smoke

OR

build stilts to be a scary giant that
roams the streets on Hallows' Eve?

WOULD YOU RATHER...

wear a cape that flips inside out to reveal a hero vs villain costume

OR

wear a hat that can grow horns from your head?

have layers of your costume peel off like a snake's skin

OR

wear mood-changing body paint?

have animal gloves with real claws attached

OR

wheels under your feet to skate through Halloween night?

WOULD YOU RATHER...

glue feathers to your face

OR

be a marshmallow monster?

make a magical floating lantern that follows you around the neighborhood

OR

a living candy collection bag?

dress up as a ballerina in a music box and have to dance in circles all night

OR

like a giant piece of bubble gum?

WOULD YOU RATHER...

dress up as a baby animal
in a furry costume

OR

dye your hair a crazy color for Halloween?

wear an alien cowboy costume

OR

a haunted superhero costume?

MYSTERY COSTUME BAG

1. Fill a bag (or box) with random costume pieces like hats, gloves, masks, scarves, or bits of fabric.
2. Each player takes a turn to reach in without looking and pull out 2–3 items.
3. Using those pieces, players must:
    - Invent a costume (however silly or spooky it looks!).
    - Create a character story to go with it.
        - Example: "I'm Captain Pumpkin Hands, and I sail a ghost ship made of candy corn!"
4. After dressing up or acting it out, share your character with the group through a quick story, funny walk, or short performance.

OPTIONAL TWIST

At the end, the group can put all the characters together into one big adventure story!

3.

HAUNTED HOUSE

Imagine you're about to go through a haunted house full of creatures and crazy things that may spook you. The only question is, *what would you rather?*

WOULD YOU RATHER...

have to walk down a creaky staircase and attract monsters in the dark with your noise

OR

battle through a hallway full of spider cobwebs?

find a secret door and explore where it goes alone

OR

a dusty library and decipher lost messages in the pages of books?

catch the eyes of a portrait moving and watching you

OR

see a haunted spinning chandelier circle above your head?

WOULD YOU RATHER...

meet a clumsy mummy

OR

a floating witch hat (with no witch!)?

talk to a skeleton

OR

a bouncing pumpkin?

be hypnotized by the glowing eyes of an owl

OR

tormented by a swarm of bats?

WOULD YOU RATHER...

hear the BANG of a door slamming shut and know you're locked inside

OR

see a chair that is rocking by itself?

discover a flickering candlelight that won't blow out

OR

footsteps without a person to link them to?

fall through a trapdoor in the floor

OR

climb into a hidden attic?

WOULD YOU RATHER...

be locked in the house with locusts and snakes

OR

locked outside in the zombie graveyard?

be possessed by a spirit that forces you to dance in a haunted ballroom

OR

hear the stories of spirits past who haunted the house?

fall through the floor into a vat of slime

OR

pool of tarantulas?

WOULD YOU RATHER...

spot a bloody handprint on the window

OR

find an eyeball rolling around the floor?

wake up when your bed starts levitating

OR

have to dine with monster guests for dinner?

find a self-playing haunted piano

OR

witches stirring bubbling cauldrons in the kitchen?

WOULD YOU RATHER...

hear mysterious chains rattling all night

OR

thunder and lightning striking the grounds outside the manor?

find a room with walls that shapeshift

OR

where the weather changes?

be trapped in a room where the walls are closing in on you

OR

be chased by monsters in a maze?

WOULD YOU RATHER...

walk into a room with monsters rehearsing a Halloween dance and join them

OR

host a Halloween karaoke night in a haunted house?

try a weird and gooey jar of eyeballs in the kitchen pantry

OR

dried mouse tails?

HAUNTED HOUSE CHARADES

1. Write spooky actions on slips of paper (or just read them out loud). Examples:
   - Walking through sticky cobwebs
   - Sneaking past a sleeping monster
   - Jumping at a loud "BANG!"
   - Tip-toeing over squeaky floorboards
2. One player picks (or is given) an action and acts it out silently. No words allowed!
3. The rest of the group guesses what they're doing.
4. Take turns until everyone has had a chance to act out different haunted house moments.

EXTRA SPOOKY TWIST

Turn off most of the lights to make the "haunted house" feel real!

HAUNTED ECHO

1. Gather everyone in a circle. One person is the "Ghost Caller."
2. The Ghost Caller says a creepy word or short phrase (like "Whooo's in the attic?" or "Beware the pumpkin king!").
3. Everyone else must repeat the phrase back in their spookiest voice—try whispering, growling, or howling like a ghost!
4. The Ghost Caller picks who gave the best (or creepiest) echo. That person becomes the next Ghost Caller.
5. Keep playing until everyone has had a turn to start a spooky echo.

EXTRA CHALLENGE

Instead of just repeating, each player must add a new spooky twist to the echo (like dragging out the last word, adding a laugh, or mixing in a monster sound). See how long you can keep the chain going!

4.

SPELL BOOK SPOOKIES

The time has come when you can cast any spell on yourself or those around you. The only question is, *what would you rather?*

WOULD YOU RATHER...

learn a spell for flying

OR

invisibility?

create a spell that hypnotizes your parents

OR

that instantly cleans your room?

cast a spell that turns your friends into water animals

OR

flying animals?

WOULD YOU RATHER...

discover a spell to grow 10x your size

OR

shrink 10x smaller?

create a silly spell that makes people laugh uncontrollably

OR

a freeze spell to stop time?

cast your spells using a sparkly wand

OR

potions you throw into the air?

WOULD YOU RATHER...

have a spell to turn any
object into a flying ride

OR

see into the future by reading
visions in a cup of water?

use the magic phrase "abracadabra"

OR

"wally wally wop" to activate your spell?

create a spell that can change the weather

OR

change your mood?

WOULD YOU RATHER...

only be able to cast spells when you wear a special crystal necklace

OR

after eating dragon soup?

use werewolf whiskers

OR

goblin snot to make a magic potion?

use the fingernail of a banshee

OR

troll sweat to make a magic potion?

WOULD YOU RATHER...

gather graveyard moss

OR

beetle wings to use in your next spell?

activate your spell with a sneeze

OR

a fart?

blow dust and everything it touches
disappears under your spell

OR

stomp 3 times and everything melts?

WOULD YOU RATHER...

toss herbs into the wind that turn into giant trampolines

OR

howl at the moon to bring all the dogs running towards you?

cough 4 times to cast a spell that silences everyone in the room

OR

sneeze 4 times to teleport to other places?

whisper your spell because it only works if no one can hear it

OR

have to write it out for it to work?

WOULD YOU RATHER...

decorate your own wand

OR

decorate your cape that must be worn to trigger your spell-casting power?

have a spell to mind control those around you

OR

read their minds?

DRAW YOUR OWN SPELL PAGE

1. Hand out a blank "spell book" page template (or just plain paper if you don't have one).
2. Each player invents a spell by:
   - Drawing magical ingredients (like dragon scales, starlight dust, or candy corn slime).
   - Writing a spell name (for example: The Giggle Potion or Broomstick Zoom).
   - Describing what happens when the spell is used. (Does it turn frogs into disco dancers? Make pumpkins sing?)
3. When everyone is finished, collect the pages to create a spell book full of silly, spooky, and magical powers.
4. Read the spells aloud together for extra laughs and "oohs" and "ahhs."

EXTRA TWIST

Everyone can "cast" one of their spells by acting it out for the group.

Magical Freeze Tag

1. Choose one player to be the Wizard. The Wizard runs around tagging others while shouting, "Freeze!"
    - When tagged, players must freeze in place like a statue.
2. Choose one player to be the Fairy or Hero. They can unfreeze players by tagging them and saying a magic word (like "Sparkle!" or "Freedom!").
3. To make it extra magical, the Wizard can shout silly effects when freezing someone:
    - "Now hop like a frog to escape!" 🐸
    - "You must tiptoe like a ghost!" 👻
    - "Flap your arms like bat wings!" 🦇
4. Keep playing until everyone has had a turn as Wizard, Fairy, or Hero.

Optional Twist

Give the Wizard a "magic wand" (like a stick, scarf, or rolled-up paper) to make their spells even more dramatic.

5.

MAGIC PETS

It's Halloween time, and you can have any kind of magical sidekick you desire. The only question is, *what would you rather?*

WOULD YOU RATHER...

have a shapeshifting grasshopper that grows big enough for you to ride it

OR

a glowing bat you can see in the dark?

have a pet ghost puppy

OR

mini fire-breathing dragon?

have a pet owl that can make it snow by flapping its wings

OR

a singing skeleton bird?

WOULD YOU RATHER...

have a pet snail that lives in a bubble

OR

a jack-o-lantern hedgehog that comes to life?

have a pet crow that's made
of Halloween candy corn

OR

a rock turtle with gemstones that
shine under the moonlight?

have a magic fairy that you keep on
a leash so they don't fly away

OR

a magic toad that turns people to stone?

WOULD YOU RATHER...

have a pet moth with ginormous wings

OR

a flying squirrel?

have a nocturnal pet (awake at night)

OR

a diurnal pet (awake during the day)?

have a magic pet that only eats boogers

OR

worms?

WOULD YOU RATHER...

have a tiny magic pet that can fit in your pocket

OR

so big you could ride your pet around the town?

have a magic pet that never sleeps

OR

one that sleeps 24/7?

have a magic pet that could cast their own spells

OR

have one special power they can use all the time?

WOULD YOU RATHER...

your magic pet was a bunny
with the roar of a lion

OR

a lion with the chirp of a bird?

have a pet raven that can see the
future but only tell it in rhymes

OR

a slug that stops people in its slime trail?

have a pet squirrel that summons lightning

OR

a pirate crab that can find
haunted buried treasure?

WOULD YOU RATHER...

have a pet piglet that oinks and dispenses candy

OR

a slithering snake that can change the color of its skin?

have a pet ferret that can walk through walls

OR

a kitten with super strength?

have a pet that can grow a tail

OR

wings?

have a magic pet that can mimic any voice

OR

see into the past?

have a magic pet that can breathe underwater

OR

has infinite strength?

GROUP PLAY

DRAW AND DESCRIBE YOUR MAGIC PET

1. Give each player a blank page with five sections:
   - Draw Your Pet ✏️
   - Pet's Name ✏️
   - Powers ✨
   - Favorite Snack 🍭
   - Special Trick 🎩
2. Each player invents their own magical creature by drawing and filling in the sections.
   - Encourage wild combos:
     - "Bat + Unicorn = Batnicorn!"
     - "Octopus + Puppy = Pupoctus!"
     - "Dragon + Hamster = Draster!"
3. When finished, everyone can share their pets with the group by introducing them, showing off drawings, and explaining their magical talents.

EXTRA OPTION

Put all the pages together to make a Magical Pet Handbook.

PET OBSTACLE COURSE

1. Set up a magical course in your space with fun "stations." Examples:
    - Flying Tunnel – crawl, wiggle, or flap through a tunnel (chairs with a blanket on top work!).
    - Glowing Bridge – balance carefully on a line of pillows, tape, or rope on the floor.
    - Candy Cave – duck under a table or crawl through a blanket fort.
2. Each player chooses a magic pet (real, silly, or invented).
3. To complete the course, they must move like their pet the whole way through!
    - Hedgehog 🦔 = crawl and curl into a ball
    - Bat 🦇 = flap arms while tip-toeing
    - Dragon 🐉 = stomp with big roars
    - Bunny 🐇 = hop, hop, hop
4. Everyone gets a turn showing off how their pet makes it through the adventure course.

EXTRA TWIST

Time each run to see which magical pet is fastest, or make it a teamwork relay where pets travel in pairs.

6.

CANDY CRAZE

Sweet, sour, and those that bestow magic powers. When you're out on Halloween night, there is an unlimited array of candy to try. The only question is *what would you rather?*

WOULD YOU RATHER...

gobble a bucket full of chocolate bars

OR

candy corn?

lick a toad-flavored lollipop

OR

slurp on a snail slushy?

munch on marshmallows

OR

tasty taffy?

WOULD YOU RATHER...

chomp on caramel apples

OR

savor sour sweets?

jump around the room eating jellybeans

OR

hiccup while drinking fizzy soda?

have bubblegum get stuck in your hair

OR

see gummy bears come alive?

WOULD YOU RATHER...

watch rock candy pop in your mouth

OR

make a straw for a milkshake using licorice?

eat peanut butter cups

OR

chocolate-covered raisins?

trick-or-treat for fortune cookies

OR

vegetables?

WOULD YOU RATHER...

take home a bag of melted fudge

OR

sour balls (so sour they make your mouth water)?

stretch taffy so far it could wrap around your whole body

OR

try butterscotch candies that are smooth and velvety on your tongue?

trick-or-treat for homemade Halloween cookies

OR

Halloween pizza?

WOULD YOU RATHER...

try creamy custard pudding in a mini jar

OR

zesty lemon candies you could
suck on for hours?

taste burnt vampire cookies

OR

creamy fish-flavored ice cream?

have salty

OR

spicy icing in a slice of Halloween cake?

WOULD YOU RATHER...

find Halloween candy from 300 years ago

OR

send your Halloween candy 300 years into the future?

make a pair of sticky slippers using Tootsie Rolls

OR

a full jewelry collection by beading candy on a string?

have all your teeth turned into jellybeans for a colorful smile

OR

your hair become sweet spaghetti taffy?

WOULD YOU RATHER...

eat a candy that gives you
the power of time travel

OR

the ability to fly like a witch on a broom?

savor candy that makes your
whole body glow-in-the-dark

OR

that gives you five-foot-long feet?

CANDY RELAY

1. Divide into teams. Each team gets a pile of candy (real or pretend).
2. Choose your tool: players must carry candy using a spoon, tongs, or scoop (no hands allowed)!
3. One at a time, players race across the room, drop their candy in a bowl or bucket, then run back to tag the next teammate.
4. Add Halloween twists for extra fun:
    - Hop like a frog 🐸
    - Walk like a mummy 🧟♂
    - Flap like a bat 🦇
    - Tiptoe like a ghost 👻
5. The first team to move all their candy wins!

EXTRA OPTION

Make it trickier. If the candy falls, the player has to start their turn over.

CANDY TOWER BUILDING

1. Gather supplies: use wrapped candies, candy bars, or small candy boxes (anything stackable).
2. Split into teams or play solo. Each group gets the same number of candies.
3. The challenge: build the tallest candy tower before the timer runs out (try 3–5 minutes).
    - No glue or tape, just balance and stack!
    - If it falls, rebuild as fast as you can.
4. When the time is up, measure which tower stands the tallest.

VARIATION

Instead of a tower, try building a Haunted Candy House with candy walls, spooky windows, and maybe even a candy ghost inside!

EXTRA TWIST

Add “haunted hazards” like a fan (wind), wobbly table, or “earthquake hands” (a teammate gently shakes the table) for a bigger challenge.

7.

MOODY MONSTERS

There are many types of creatures and ghouls to meet out on Hallows' Eve. The only question is, *what would you rather?*

WOULD YOU RATHER...

meet a werewolf chasing their tail under the moon

OR

a sinister doll with stitches across her face?

run into tickle trolls that will make you laugh for hours

OR

sleepy giants with snores so loud they shake the ground?

bump into a grumpy ogre

OR

a lonely skeleton?

WOULD YOU RATHER...

get to know a shy witch

OR

a nervous mummy?

dine with a friendly fanged vampire

OR

winged fairy?

befriend a cute Cyclops

OR

a floating hand (with no body!)?

WOULD YOU RATHER...

chase a zombie zooming around the neighborhood

OR

feast with Frankenstein and eat dead mice?

ride horses under the stars with the Headless Horseman

OR

roll down hills at night with smurfs?

giggle with the Grim Reaper

OR

drink hot cocoa with Dracula?

WOULD YOU RATHER...

go for a graveyard walk with ghosts

OR

ask talking pumpkin heads about the craziest thing they've ever seen?

learn to hang upside down like a bat

OR

spin webs like a spider?

play hide and seek with pixies

OR

shadow monsters?

WOULD YOU RATHER...

bake cookies with a banshee

OR

watch a scarecrow come to life?

eat candy with a creepy clown

OR

cast spells with an evil sorcerer?

meet a monster with super strength

OR

super speed?

WOULD YOU RATHER...

befriend a monster that shows
you how to mind-read

OR

predicts the future?

spend a day living with a monster family

OR

bring a monster home to your family?

join a monster band and tour
the town for Halloween

OR

meet the famous Phantom of the Opera?

meet mermaids that take you around a haunted lake

OR

ghosts that live in lakeside caverns?

stumble upon a mad scientist in the middle of his newest experiment

OR

enchanted fairies causing mayhem?

DESIGN A MONSTER TRADING CARD

1. Give each player a blank card template (or cut paper into card-sized rectangles).
2. On each card, design your own monster by filling in:
   - Picture – Draw your monster.
   - Name – Give it a spooky, silly, or powerful name.
   - Mood – Is it grumpy, silly, sneaky, sleepy?
   - Power Level – Rank it from 1 to 10.
   - Favorite Trick or Candy – What does it love most?
3. Once finished, everyone can share their monster cards with the group, then trade or combine them to make monster teams.

EXTRA OPTION

Create a Monster Battle Game. Monsters face off by comparing power levels, moods, or favorite tricks.

MONSTER SOUND ORCHESTRA

1. Assign each player a monster sound. Examples:
   - "BOO!" 👻
   - "HOWL!" 🐺
   - "CLANK!" ⚙️
   - "MWA-HA-HA!" 😈
   - "SLURP!" 🧟
2. One player is the Conductor. The Conductor points to the other players to make their sound.
3. The Conductor can change how the sounds are made:
   - Quiet or Loud
   - Fast or Slow
   - One at a time or all together
4. Keep going until you've built a full monster symphony of silly-spooky sounds!
5. Switch conductors so everyone gets a turn leading the orchestra.

EXTRA TWIST

Record the "monster music" and play it back. Now listen to your haunted house band!

8.

PUMPKIN CARVING COMPETITION

This tradition of Halloween calls on you to use your creativity and imagination to design and bring to life a pumpkin from your greatest nightmare! The only question is, ***what would you rather?***

WOULD YOU RATHER...

scoop out the pumpkin seeds
and roast them to eat

OR

make a body scrub from them?

stencil a pumpkin design to carve

OR

paint on a pumpkin face instead?

have a candle with a real
flame burning inside

OR

color-changing LED lights to shine
through your pumpkin's face?

WOULD YOU RATHER...

use toothpicks for teeth in the smile of your pumpkin

OR

fingernail clippings?

carve a pumpkin family of three that stack on top of each other

OR

one giant pumpkin?

carve a pumpkin that looks angry

OR

sad?

WOULD YOU RATHER...

carve a pumpkin that looks scary

OR

is laughing?

add little hearts and diamonds

OR

moon and star cutouts to your pumpkin?

give your pumpkin a crown

OR

a cape?

WOULD YOU RATHER...

customize your pumpkin with triangle

OR

squinty eyes?

have a button nose

OR

a long carrot nose on your pumpkin?

have a pumpkin-carving night
with your friends

OR

family?

WOULD YOU RATHER...

carve a scene of ghosts and witches on your pumpkin

OR

superheroes?

decorate your pumpkin with candy earrings

OR

glow-in-the-dark paint?

use a pumpkin that's tall and oblong

OR

short and stout?

WOULD YOU RATHER...

use a pumpkin that has a rough texture

OR

is smooth to the touch?

use the insides of the pumpkin to create crazy hair near its horn

OR

hair from its ears?

cover your pumpkin in glitter

OR

silly string cobwebs?

WOULD YOU RATHER...

give your pumpkin a silly headband

OR

tree-branch arms?

put a voice recorder with spooky messages in your pumpkin

OR

a smoke machine?

GROUP PLAY

GUESS THAT PUMPKIN FACE

1. Show pumpkin face silhouettes (print or draw a few on paper/board). Each one should have a different expression: angry, happy, silly, surprised, spooky.
2. Players take turns guessing the mood of each pumpkin.
    - Example: "That one looks scared!" or "That pumpkin is definitely laughing!"
3. After guessing, each player draws their own pumpkin face to match the mood.
    - Encourage creativity: big teeth, funny eyes, wiggly mouths, or even extra features like bat ears or witch hats.
4. Share the pumpkin faces with the group and see how many wild and funny expressions everyone came up with!

EXTRA TWIST

Make it a challenge round where one player acts out the mood of the pumpkin, and the others guess.

STEP-BY-STEP PUMPKIN CARVING

Important: Always have an adult help with sharp tools.

1. Pick Your Pumpkin
    - Choose a medium-sized pumpkin that's not too soft.
2. Prepare Your Space
    - Cover the table with a newspaper or an old cloth.
    - Have bowls ready for pumpkin seeds and "guts."
3. Cut the Lid (Adult Job)
    - An adult carefully cuts around the stem to make a lid.
    - Scoop off any seeds stuck underneath.
4. Scoop It Out
    - Use a big spoon to scoop out seeds and stringy pulp.
    - Save the seeds if you want to roast them later!
5. Draw Your Face
    - Using a marker, sketch the pumpkin's face (happy, scary, silly, surprised).
    - Add extra details like stars, cats, or lightning bolts.

6. Carve the Design (Adult Job)
    - Adults carefully cut along the drawn lines.
    - Brush away scraps and hold the pumpkin steady.
7. Light It Up
    - Place a tea light candle inside (battery candles are safest).
    - Put the lid back on and admire your glowing creation!

EXTRA OPTIONS

- Instead of cutting, paint or decorate the pumpkin with stickers for a no-knife version.
- Host a Pumpkin Parade: line up everyone's pumpkins and give each one a fun name.

9.

MYTHS AT MIDNIGHT

Halloween myths and legends have been around for centuries, across cultures and countries. As you dive into some spooky scenarios, the only question is, *what would you rather?*

WOULD YOU RATHER...

be stranded in Dracula's castle
with the vampire himself

OR

snatched up by the Headless Horseman
and carried off into the night?

be chased by a werewolf through the woods

OR

have your spirit stuck in a jack-
o-lantern for all of time?

be a witch's prisoner

OR

apprentice?

WOULD YOU RATHER...

be eaten by a ghost

OR

attacked by a black cat?

take in a black cat but be struck with bad luck for 10 years

OR

be cursed as a werewolf that changes under every full moon?

follow a mysterious floating lantern deep in the woods

OR

be followed by a shadow creature?

WOULD YOU RATHER...

see a pair of glowing eyes in the dark

OR

a face in the mist?

hear a spooky laugh from something following you

OR

footsteps echoing down the hallway?

live in a haunted forest

OR

creaky old library?

WOULD YOU RATHER...

learn a witch's spell

OR

have your own haunted house?

travel to a spooky castle and meet Dracula

OR

a long-lost princess?

bump into a talking pumpkin

OR

a floating witch's hat?

WOULD YOU RATHER...

open a haunted book and get sucked into the story

OR

bring the characters into the real world?

follow a ghost dog

OR

a tiny goblin?

be swallowed by a magic box

OR

be cursed with invisibility so no one could see you ever again?

WOULD YOU RATHER...

meet a three-headed dog

OR

the Loch Ness Monster?

have a crow pick you up and fly off with you

OR

get a mysterious phone call from a monster?

find a dragon scale

OR

a map to the underworld?

WOULD YOU RATHER...

learn to play a bone flute
that summons zombies

OR

have a moonstone amulet that
controls an army of black cats?

be given a witch's broom

OR

a silver dagger?

MONSTER FOOTPRINT HUNT

LEGEND

Monsters leave behind giant tracks wherever they go. Can you follow them?

1. Make the footprints – Cut out big monster feet from cardboard or paper. Decorate them with claws, slime, or glitter!
2. Set the trail – A player hides the footprints around the room, yard, or garden. Place them in a path that leads to a final surprise (like a hidden "monster," treasure chest, or treat bag).
3. Start the hunt! – The other players follow the trail of monster tracks, step by step, searching for the end.
4. Find the treasure – At the last footprint, discover the monster's hiding spot or a treasure (candy, stickers, glow sticks, or even a silly monster mask).

EXTRA TWISTS

- **Multiple monsters:** Use different colors or shapes of footprints to represent different creatures.
- **Clue cards:** Add riddles or mini challenges along the way.
- **Night hunt:** Make glow-in-the-dark footprints with glow-in-the-dark pens for a spooky version!

CYCLOPS EYE TOSS

LEGEND

A Cyclops only has one giant eye. Can you toss it back where it belongs?

1. Set up the target – Use a cauldron, bucket, or cardboard monster mouth as the "eye socket."
2. Get the eyes ready – Use ping pong balls, soft foam balls, or balled-up paper as the Cyclops's eyes. You can even draw eyeballs on them with markers for extra fun!
3. Take turns tossing – Players stand a few feet away and toss the eyes into the target.
4. Level up the challenge:
    - Level 1: Toss from close up.
    - Level 2: Take a step back.
    - Level 3: Toss while hopping on one foot.
    - Level 4: Toss blindfolded or with eyes closed for a real Cyclops challenge.
5. Keep score or just play for fun. See who can land the most eyes in the cauldron!

EXTRA TWIST

Paint or decorate the bucket/cauldron like a monster face so it looks like the eyes are going right back in its head!

10. CREEPY CRAWLIES

Bugs, critters, and tiny creatures of the woods are all showing up in different situations. The only question is, *what would you rather?*

WOULD YOU RATHER...

fall into a vat of spiders

OR

beetles?

taste centipede candy

OR

shaped like a cockroach head?

make moth soup

OR

a cricket cocktail?

WOULD YOU RATHER...

fry flies on a barbecue

OR

watch worms wiggle in a soup?

wear a stinkbug necklace

OR

ladybug earrings?

walk past fire ants

OR

mosquitoes?

WOULD YOU RATHER...

have butterfly earrings

OR

a tarantula for a ring?

have dragonflies follow you around

OR

larvae stick to your room's door?

find an enchanted mirror that will grant you any wish, but turns you into a bug

OR

find a charm bag full of magic dust and larvae?

WOULD YOU RATHER...

make a sandwich from worm paste

OR

make a slug smoothie?

be stuck in a giant spider web

OR

have ants living in your room?

your hair turned into a cricket nest

OR

your Halloween costume was made out of live grasshoppers?

WOULD YOU RATHER...

have to swim through a pool of flies

OR

mosquitoes?

reach into your dresser and come out with a handful of tarantulas

OR

beetle dung?

use live dragonflies

OR

butterflies as decorative hair accessories?

WOULD YOU RATHER...

find a family of bugs wearing top hats inside your winter boots

OR

in the refrigerator?

find a family of bugs surfing in a bubbling cauldron of slime

OR

ice skating on the frozen punch bowl at a Halloween party?

drink spider milk (made by the Toxeus spider)

OR

have spider eggs on crackers?

WOULD YOU RATHER...

spot a caterpillar on the end of your toothbrush

OR

crawling out of the faucet?

be able to hear beetles fart (like the Bombardier beetle)

OR

use your own farts to ward off all bugs?

SPIDER WEB MAZE

1. **Build the web:** Use yarn, string, or streamers to crisscross a hallway, doorway, or between trees outside. Make sure to vary the heights so players have to crawl under, duck through, and climb over.
2. **Set the challenge:** The web belongs to a giant sleeping spider (assign someone to this role). If you touch the strands, the spider might wake up!
3. **Take turns through the maze:** Players move one at a time, carefully making their way through without touching the web.
4. **Add difficulty (optional):**
    - Time each run to see who is the fastest.
    - Bring a small "treasure" (like a candy or token) to carry through without dropping.
    - Add a "spider guard" (another player) who can clap or hiss if they see someone touch the web!
5. Everyone wins once they escape the maze without waking the spider.

EXTRA TWIST

Play in dim light with a flashlight for extra creepy, nighttime vibes.

GROUP PLAY

ANT TRAIL CHALLENGE

1. **Create the trail:** Use tape, paper footprints, or colorful dots on the floor to make a winding path like an ant trail.
2. **Get your ant snack:** Each player balances a candy corn (or a small toy bug) on a spoon.
3. **Walk the trail:** Players must carefully follow the path without dropping their "ant snack."
4. If it falls, stop, place it back on the spoon, and continue.
5. **Challenge modes:**
    - Race against the clock
    - Relay race in teams
    - Walk like ants (tiny steps, hands up, or crawling!)

EXTRA TWIST

At the end of the trail, place an "ant hill" bucket where players must drop their snack to finish the challenge.

11.

NOT-SO-GORY GAMES

Some of the best parts of Halloween are the spine-chilling and spooktacular games you get to play with friends and family. The only question is, *what would you rather?*

WOULD YOU RATHER...

go apple bopping with a blindfold

OR

play pumpkin toss and see who can throw the furthest?

have a race to wrap your friends up like a mummy

OR

eat the most candy corn in 5 minutes?

go through a hay bale maze

OR

bowling with pumpkins?

WOULD YOU RATHER...

have a relay race balancing a witch hat on your head

OR

a costume parade with a trophy for the best in show?

play Halloween bingo

OR

create a Halloween treasure hunt?

pin the fang on the vampire

OR

bat at a Halloween piñata?

WOULD YOU RATHER...

play freeze dance with zombies

OR

have a creepy cook-off with Halloween cakes and bakes?

play ping pong with eyeballs

OR

see who can balance a magic wand the longest on their ear?

host a karaoke night with all the ghouls and ghosts you can imagine

OR

have a costume designing competition?

WOULD YOU RATHER...

play glow stick hide-and-seek

OR

jack-o-lantern toss (don't let it drop!)?

play mini golf

OR

baseball with tiny pumpkins?

play laser tag with Darth Vader

OR

a stormtrooper?

WOULD YOU RATHER...

have to walk a tightrope
over a vat of snakes

OR

spiders?

have a bake-off and try creepy desserts

OR

cook-off and try main dishes blindfolded?

play catch-the-bug with your
tongue and catch flies

OR

worms?

WOULD YOU RATHER...

create stink-bug perfumes and compete for the worst smell

OR

a blanket-weaving competition using monster hair?

see who can balance an eyeball on their hand the longest

OR

who can carve the most pumpkins in under 5 minutes?

divide your party into teams for the games

OR

have everyone compete individually?

WOULD YOU RATHER...

make player jerseys

OR

create spooktacular player names for your scoreboards?

win a lifetime supply of candy

OR

a magic potion made to order?

MUMMY WRAP RACE

1. Split into teams of 3–5 players. Each team chooses one person to be the Mummy.
2. On "Go!", teammates race to wrap the Mummy from head to toe using toilet paper.
    - Wrap gently (don't cover the face)!
    - Make sure arms and legs get wrapped for a spooky mummy look.
3. The first team to finish a complete mummy wrap wins!
4. When the race is done, carefully unwrap the Mummy and roll the toilet paper back up to avoid waste.

EXTRA TWISTS

- **Walking Mummies:** Once wrapped, the Mummy must wobble to the finish line without the paper falling off.
- **Best Dressed Mummy:** Instead of racing, vote on the funniest, scariest, or silliest Mummy wrap.

PIN THE FANGS ON THE VAMPIRE

1. **Set up the vampire:** Hang up a big poster or drawing of a vampire without fangs.
2. **Make the fangs:** Cut out paper fangs (one for each player). Write their name or give each set a different color so you know whose is whose.
3. **Blindfold the player:** Spin them around 2–3 times for extra fun.
4. **Pin the fangs!** Players try to stick their fangs as close to the vampire's mouth as possible.
5. **Winner:** The player whose fangs land closest to the right spot wins!

EXTRA TWISTS

- Use tape or sticky tack so fangs stay in place.
- Give the vampire silly accessories too (like bats, mustaches, or candy) for bonus rounds.
- Make a "Pin the Hat on the Witch" or "Pin the Eye on the Cyclops" version for variety.

12. PARTY PLANNING

It's your turn to throw a Halloween bash and make it a special monster mash! The only question is, *what would you rather?*

WOULD YOU RATHER...

have a classic haunted house party

OR

a monster mash dance party?

host a Candy Land carnival

OR

a costume ball?

have a mad scientist lab party

OR

a trick-or-treat treasure hunt?

WOULD YOU RATHER...

hang glow sticks

OR

fairy lights for decor?

have black and orange balloons

OR

streamers?

have a fog machine

OR

disco ball?

offer face painting

OR

washable tattoos at the party?

have a magic show

OR

a puppet show for all to watch?

have spooky storytelling sessions

OR

a dance-off?

WOULD YOU RATHER...

have a limbo competition

OR

a talent show?

serve witch's brew with floating eyeballs

OR

ghost-shaped sandwiches with worms?

serve pizza with spider web toppings

OR

glow-in-the-dark jelly?

WOULD YOU RATHER...

HALLOWEEN

31

have spooky sound effects
playing when people enter

OR

songs from your favorite Halloween movies?

invite a select group of friends

OR

open the party up to your
whole neighborhood?

make party favors

OR

have a photo booth for a take-
home memory of the night?

HALLOWEEN

WOULD YOU RATHER...

play games for prizes

OR

truth or dare?

draw special invitations

OR

send a video invite to guests?

follow a dress code

OR

guests could wear whatever they want?

WOULD YOU RATHER...

HALLOWEEN

have a DJ

OR

a live band?

host the party during the day

OR

at night?

PLAN A HALLOWEEN SNACK MENU

1. Gather the group and give each player a piece of paper and pen/pencil.
2. Together, brainstorm spooky snacks and drinks you could serve at a Halloween party.
    - Examples:
        - Witch's Brew Punch
        - Monster Eyeball Cupcakes
        - Pumpkin Pizzas
        - Ghost Popcorn Bags
        - Bloody Red Juice (cranberry or cherry)
3. Each player writes or draws at least one treat idea for the menu.
4. Collect all the ideas and create a group snack menu. Decorate it with spooky doodles, slime borders, or bat wings.
5. Read the menu aloud like you're at a fancy Halloween restaurant!

EXTRA TWISTS

- Vote on the "spookiest snack" or "funniest food name."
- If you have time, pick one idea to actually make together.

CREATE A PARTY PLAYLIST

1. Give each player a turn to pick a favorite Halloween song (or spooky-silly song).
    - Examples: monster, ghost, or witch-themed songs.
2. Write all the choices down to create a Halloween Party Playlist.
3. Play the songs in order and let everyone dance, sing, or act out the music.
4. For extra fun, vote on:
    - Best dance moves
    - Scariest performance
    - Funniest monster impression

EXTRA TWIST

Pretend the playlist is a radio station. One player can be the "DJ" and introduce each song in their spookiest or silliest voice.

13.

MONSTER MENU

You're about to meet some monsters who have the munchies, and it's up to you to choose the dishes to serve them! The only question is, *what would you rather?*

WOULD YOU RATHER...

serve slime-covered sandwiches

OR

smelly smoothies?

offer monster mucus dip

OR

squishy eyeball jelly?

try bone breadsticks

OR

oozy eyeball cupcakes?

WOULD YOU RATHER...

snack on creepy crawly pizza with bug toppings

OR

crunchy cockroach cookies?

slurp on brain jelly

OR

toenail fries?

serve finger sandwiches made from real fingers (!)

OR

ogre sweat stew?

WOULD YOU RATHER...

make swamp juice cider

OR

Dracula's blood bunch?

have pickled rat tails

OR

graveyard dirt as an appetizer?

your main dish is farting frog fritters

OR

baked ziti made from zombies?

WOULD YOU RATHER...

make spider egg salad

OR

hairy finger french fries?

offer moth-wing muffins for breakfast

OR

bone-crunch cereal?

serve earwax fudge

OR

a crunchy cockroach cake?

WOULD YOU RATHER...

offer a bat blood latte

OR

ogre breath soda?

make rice crispy treats with beetle fluff

OR

caterpillar hair?

try roasted tarantula toes

OR

centipede sushi rolls?

WOULD YOU RATHER...

have a side of caterpillar coleslaw

OR

cricket cornbread?

make pill bug potatoes

OR

flea fried rice?

have maggot mousse

OR

mosquito milkshakes for dessert?

WOULD YOU RATHER...

serve chocolate-covered cockroach clusters

OR

mealworm meatballs?

stir up beetles with beans

OR

termite toast?

MONSTER FOOD POETRY

1. Give each player a pen and paper (or a notebook).
2. Together, brainstorm some gross monster meals to inspire poems.

   Examples:

   - Worm Spaghetti
   - Slime Soup
   - Bat Wing Brownies
   - Swampy Swirl Smoothie
   - Pickled Dragon Toes
   - Eyeball Ice Cream
3. Each player picks one (or invents their own!) and writes a silly or spooky poem about it.
   - Short and funny poems work great (rhyming couplets, limericks, or even a spooky haiku).
4. When done, read your poems aloud to the group in your scariest, funniest, or most dramatic monster voice.

EXTRA TWIST

Collect all the poems into a Monster Menu Poetry Book and decorate it with doodles of the foods.

DRAW YOUR CRAZIEST MONSTER MENU ITEM

1. Give each player a page and some pencils/markers.
2. Ask them to invent the wildest, grossest, or silliest monster food they can imagine.
    - Examples:
        - Spaghetti with Spider Legs
        - Slime Sundae with Eyeball Sprinkles
        - Pumpkin Guts Pizza
        - Worm Burrito with Swamp Sauce
3. On the page, they should:
    - Draw their monster meal in as much detail as possible.
    - Write a name for their dish.
    - Describe how to make it (real recipe steps or silly monster-style cooking).
    - Explain what it tastes like (delicious, disgusting, magical, surprising).
4. Once finished, everyone can share their creations by reading aloud the recipe and showing their drawing.

EXTRA TWIST

Collect everyone's pages to make a Monster Cookbook for the group!

14.

FLYING THROUGH THE SKY

On Halloween night, many different spooky, wacky, funny, and bizarre things can be seen flying through the night. The only question is, *what would you rather?*

WOULD YOU RATHER...

see witches on broomsticks

OR

ghosts floating softly through the sky?

spot bats swooping and swirling

OR

owls with glowing eyes?

witness a dragon breathing fire

OR

fairies with sparkling wings?

WOULD YOU RATHER...

observe vampires flying silently

OR

E.T. with his other alien friends?

notice flying pumpkins with faces

OR

black cats leaping through the air?

lay eyes on living gargoyles guarding stone buildings

OR

magic flying carpets?

WOULD YOU RATHER...

witness a glowing spaceship
come down to earth

OR

flying squirrels soaring through the sky?

notice a pirate ghost ship
sailing through the sky

OR

aliens riding shooting stars?

watch a haunted hot air balloon
float above your neighborhood

OR

a swarm of locusts covering the whole sky?

WOULD YOU RATHER...

notice faint writing in the sky and have to decode the message

OR

floating skeletons playing violins?

spot an army of grim reapers all flying towards your home

OR

zombie parrots?

go stargazing and see the famous edge of the Milky Way galaxy

OR

a full moon?

WOULD YOU RATHER...

witness the ancient Greek gods
come to life and battle in the night sky

OR

see Santa with his reindeer?

spy a Cyclops with a jetpack

OR

werewolves with wings?

see a haunted coffin with bat wings

OR

mummies parasailing with their own wrappings?

WOULD YOU RATHER...

spot a shimmering ghost train chugging through the stars

OR

floating crystal balls projecting spooky visions?

witness stars rearranging themselves into creepy faces

OR

a glowing doorway hanging in the air, calling you to go in?

see clouds shaped like monsters

OR

haunted castles?

WOULD YOU RATHER...

watch Halloween hot air balloons drift by

OR

an alien spaceship?

watch a brigade of witches race each other across the night sky

OR

flying vampires?

CREATE A NIGHT SKY SCENE

1. Give each player a blank sheet of paper (black paper works best!) and art supplies (crayons, markers, scissors, glue, or magazines for collage).
2. Each player can create their own Halloween night sky, filled with:
   - A glowing moon
   - Bright stars or even spooky constellations
   - Flying creatures like bats, witches, owls, or ghosts
   - Clouds, shooting stars, or magical swirls
3. Draw, cut and paste, or mix both styles to bring your sky to life.
4. When everyone's finished, display the skies together to make one giant "Haunted Galaxy Wall."

EXTRA TWIST

Add glow-in-the-dark stickers, glitter, or foil scraps so the skies really shine when the lights go out!

MAKE FLYING CREATURE MASKS

1. Give each player supplies, like paper plates, cardstock, scissors, markers, string, glue, and any decorations (feathers, glitter, fabric scraps).
2. Each player chooses a flying Halloween creature to make into a mask or hat, such as:
    - Bat 🦇
    - Owl 🦉
    - Witch on a broom 🧙‍♀️
    - Ghost 👻
    - Dragon 🐉
3. Each player designs and decorates their masks:
    - Cut out holes for eyes.
    - Add ears, wings, or hats with extra paper.
    - Attach a string or elastic to wear it.
4. Once everyone's finished, put on the masks and pretend to fly around together, flapping, swooping, or gliding across the room!

EXTRA TWIST

Host a Flying Creature Parade where each player shows off their mask and makes their best creature sounds or flying moves.

15.

CREATE YOUR OWN QUESTIONS!

Now it's your turn to think of the craziest, funniest, wackiest, scariest, mind-blowing questions. Use the Word Bank on the next page to write your own WOULD YOU RATHER questions.

WORD BANK

GENERAL HALLOWEEN WORDS

pumpkin • costume • candy • trick-or-treat • ghost • monster • haunted house • witch • broomstick • bat • black cat • spooky • scare • cobweb • skeleton • vampire • zombie • goblin • creepy • eerie • jack-o'-lantern • spider • full moon • boo • cauldron • lantern • potion

HALLOWEEN NIGHT & ATMOSPHERE

moonlight • fog • shadows • dark sky • glowing eyes • howling wind • creaky floor • whispering trees • candlelight • eerie silence • haunted whispers • thunder • lightning • graveyard • fog machine • starless sky • midnight • rustling leaves • sudden chill • owl hoot

CREATURES, CHARACTERS & COSTUMES

witch • wizard • vampire • mummy • werewolf • ghost • zombie • fairy • alien • monster • skeleton • Frankenstein • clown • robot • scarecrow • devil • angel • superhero • pirate • pumpkin head • mad scientist • enchanted creature • creepy doll • bat boy • spider queen

MAGIC, POTIONS & SPELLS

cauldron • wand • spell book • potion bottle • bubbling brew • curse • enchantment • magic dust • broomstick flight • invisibility spell • transformation charm • glowing vial • talking mirror • magic hat • sparkle burst • spell-casting • charm chant • elixir • crystal orb • cursed scroll

WORD BANK

HAUNTED HOUSE & SPOOKY SURPRISES

creaky stairs • cobwebs • dusty books • moving portraits • glowing eyes • secret door • trapdoor • spooky attic • haunted hallway • ghost in the mirror • levitating objects • bats in the rafters • whispering voices • skeleton in the closet • shadowy figure • thumping footsteps • broken chandelier • ghostly music • flying furniture • hidden room

CANDY & TREATS

candy corn • chocolate bar • gummy worms • lollipops • caramel apples • sour candy • jellybeans • licorice • spooky cupcakes • candy eyeballs • toffee • marshmallow ghosts • peanut butter cups • popcorn balls • trick-or-treat bag • sugar rush • spooky cookies • monster mash mix • haunted snack bowl

CREEPY CRAWLIES & CRITTERS

spider • bat • black cat • rat • cockroach • beetle • centipede • worm • snake • toad • moth • skeleton bird • slime bug • glowing beetle • invisible insect • vampire bat • dusty web • bug in your candy • creepy scuttle • tickly feet

WORD BANK

ACTION WORDS & HALLOWEEN VERBS

screaming • giggling • hiding • running • chasing • cackling • haunting • flying • creeping • crawling • slithering • jumping • tiptoeing • casting • transforming • glowing • vanishing • sneaking • bubbling • brewing • spooking • rattling • shrieking • knocking • knocking again!

FEELINGS, MOODS & REACTIONS

scared • brave • silly • surprised • excited • spooked • jumpy • nervous • curious • sneaky • wild • giggly • creeped-out • brave-faced • thrilled • enchanted • goofy • daring • jittery • chilled • thrilled • bold • mystified • wide-eyed

HALLOWEEN PLAY & IMAGINATION

costume contest • haunted maze • trick-or-treat race • monster dance-off • scary story circle • candy trading table • make-your-own-potion station • spooky scavenger hunt • pumpkin relay race • guess-the-creature game • invisible costume game • slime lab • creepy crafts corner • cardboard coffin photo booth • pumpkin patch pretend • broomstick obstacle course • monster mash freeze dance

WOULD YOU RATHER...

OR

OR

OR

WOULD YOU RATHER...

OR

OR

OR

WOULD YOU RATHER...

OR

OR

OR

WOULD YOU RATHER...

OR

OR

OR

WOULD YOU RATHER...

OR

OR

OR

WOULD YOU RATHER...

OR

OR

OR

WOULD YOU RATHER...

OR

OR

OR

WOULD YOU RATHER...

OR

OR

OR

CONCLUSION

Goolia the Ghost again. Wow, you made it all the way to the end and generated some powerful decision-making skills in the process!

Now that you've made it through mind-bending questions and fantastical scenarios, take a moment to reflect on all the questions you've answered, the things you've learned about those you played with, and the situations you created on your own in the last section.

Did this book inspire you to be silly?

Did you laugh with your friends and family?

What was the favorite thing you learned about the world or yourself along the way?

Remember to stay curious and never shy away from your imagination! Your imagination is a gateway for creative problem-solving that the world needs.

Printed in Dunstable, United Kingdom

67378182R00090

Provisional Avant-Gardes

Post45
Kate Marshall and Loren Glass, Editors
Post•45 Group, Editorial Committee